25 Quick Tips for Creating Memorable

Customer Appreciation
Events

in Order to Maximize Profits and Create

Fast Small Business Success!

Collin Stover

25 Quick Tips for Creating Memorable Customer Appreciation Events in Order to Maximize Profits and Create Fast Small Business Success! by Collin Stover

Interior Separation Design by: http://all-silhouettes.com/flourishornaments/
Cover icons by Freekpik from www.flaticon.com are licensed under Creative Commons BY 3.0
Publisher: Collin Stover
ISBN: 978-1-312-96576-8
1. Business 2. Marketing
Second Edition

CONTENTS

Introduction..1
Tip #1: How to Calculate the Potential Value of
an Event..6
Tip #2: 4 Ways to Make Money From an Event...........10
Tip #3: Design the Event for Sponsors......................13
Tip #4: ...But be Sneaky About It...............................17
Tip #5: Theme It...18
Tip #6: Invest in an Event Planner.............................20
Tip #7: The First Step is Visualization......................22
Tip #8: Leave Nothing to Chance (But Be Flexible)....23
Tip #9: Book the Venue First
(Then Entertainment)..26
Tip #10: How to Avoid Being ROBBED by Vendors....29
Tip #11: The Pros and Cons of Working With
Talent Agencies...32
Tip #12: The Best Times to Have an Event..................36
Tip #13: Who to Invite..39
Tip #14: Paper Invitations vs. E-Vites.......................40
Tip #15: What to Include on Invitations.....................41
Tip #16: Follow Up with Your Invitees.......................46
Tip #17: Use Ambiance to Create an Unforgettable
Sensory Experience...49
Tip #18: Keep Education Interesting..........................51
Tip #19: Include Something for Everyone....................52
Tip #20: Craft a Grand Entrance.................................53
Tip #21: Entertain them While They're There.............56
Tip #22: Say Goodbye (the Right Way)!......................59

Tip #23: Say Thank You...59

Tip #24: Measure the Success of Your Event.................61

Tip #25: Claim the Most Amazing Free Gift Ever!........64

About the Author: Collin Stover..66

Over the past ten years, I have performed at events as a magician and mentalist for thousands of individuals: from small business owners, to executives of large corporations, to celebrities, and to NHL and NFL superstars. Companies routinely put their trust in my expertise to ensure that the events they plan for their customers, employees, and important vendors are entertaining and extremely successful.

It's over these ten years of performing that I have learned a thing or two about what makes an event successful, and what companies should look to avoid if they aren't keen on wasting money and driving away customers.

I didn't go to school to become an event planner,

nor do I belong to any event planning associations. Frankly, all of my experience is based on the countless events I've been a part of, my own experience with planning my annual customer appreciation event, and interviews I've conducted with dozens of event experts, vendors, and my own clients. It's because of this that I've left out a lot of the confusing jargon that often accompanies books of this nature, in order to only give you what is absolutely necessary for planning and executing a successful customer appreciation event. After all, you don't want to be an event planner, do you? If so, there are some great courses for you to take, but this is not in that category.

No, this book is for the small business owner. The one who throws 1-4 events per year to show appreciation for their customers, team, and/or important vendors, and is looking to maximize their profits and create fast business success.

Let's get something straight: I don't invest in a single marketing effort in my business that I can't track, measure, and hold accountable for results. I won't put an ad out without a call to action, I won't use social media without utilizing tools to measure its effectiveness, and I won't host an event unless I have a clear way of measuring my success (or failure).

That's part of the reason I wrote this book. There are so many businesses out there that haphazardly throw together events for their customers without any thought to how to maximize or even measure their return on investment.

In the book, *How You Do...What You Do: Create Service Excellence That Wins Clients for Life* by Bob Livingston, CEO of sales consulting group REL Communications, Mr. Livingston lists the **5 reasons customers stop doing patronizing most businesses:**

- 1% pass away

- 3% move

- 14% are lured away by a competitor

- 14% are turned away by product or service dissatisfaction

- **And a whopping 68% leave because of poor attitude or indifference on the part of the service provider!**

Unfortunately, this means that for at least 18% of the customers who stop doing business with you, there is little you can do to keep them here, spending money with you.

The great news is that you are in complete control of 82% of the customers who take that proverbial plunge.

The even better news here is that for the 68% who fall in the last category, you didn't do anything *wrong*, per se. You just didn't do anything *extra* to make them feel appreciated or to keep them from getting bored.

Part of the solution to this is planning an event for all of your customers to show them just how much they're appreciated by you and your business.

This isn't rocket science. The idea here is quite simple: when customers feel appreciated and recognized by your business, they feel the need to reciprocate. They do so in a variety of ways: with referrals, with increased number of purchases, and with decreased resistance to price.

My stepfather always told me that if something is worth doing, it's worth doing right. That is what this book is about. It's about making the choice between "winging it" and expertly choreographing an event that your customers won't soon forget.

After all, what business wants to be forgotten?

Tip #1: How to Calculate the Potential Value of an Event

How does the 68% number I mentioned in the introduction translate into dollars and cents being lost by your business? I'm about to hit you with some math, so get ready. The numbers don't lie.

The first step is knowing the lifetime value of your average customer. A *brief* version of this formula, not factoring in referrals, is: Average price of sale x average number of times a customer does business with you per year x the average number of years a customer stays with your business x your profit margin = the lifetime value of the average customer. Then you need to know how many people leave your business every year.

Using these two numbers, you can calculate exactly how much money is being left on the table by those customers who don't feel quite appreciated enough.

Take Tracy's Floral, for example, on the next page. Here were Tracy's stats before she started hosting events:

	Tracy's Floral
Average Price Per Sale	$25
Average # of Sales/Year/Customer	4
Average # of Years a Customer Stays w/ Business	5
Profit Margins (Gross Profit from a Sale)	50%
Average Lifetime Value of a Customer (Multiply all of the above)	**$250**

Now lets say that every year, 10% of Tracy's customers hit that 5 year mark and stop doing business with her, and let's say that she usually has an active customer list of 200 customers.

This means that on average per year, 20 customers will disappear into thin air ($5000 – how frustrating)!

Because we know the average percentages for why customers stop doing business with a company, we can estimate that 14 customers (68% of 20, rounded) are leaving each year because Tracy isn't making them feel quite appreciated enough.

That's $3500 being left on the table each year due to a feeling of indifference alone! Over 10 years, that is of course $35,000. I'm sure Tracy could use that extra money for bills, college for her kids, or a nice vacation every year.

I'm not a math person, so I can appreciate that doing these calculations for your business can seem like a headache. But I *am* a business person, and as such, I enjoy maximizing my profits, and I take notice when thousands of dollars are being left on the table year after year. **That's why I want to urge you to figure this out for your own business.**

I've made it easy for you by providing you with the table below and on the next page. Simply fill in the numbers for your own business (you can use a calculator!) to see how much extra money you could potentially save by putting together an appreciation event.

	Florist	Clothing Store	You
Average Price Per Sale	$25	$500	
Average # of Sales/ Year/Customer	4	2	
Average # of Years a Customer Stays w/ Business	5	6	

Profit Margins (Gross Profit from a Sale)	50%	40%	
Average Lifetime Value of a Customer (Multiply the Above)	$250	$2400	
Number of Total Customers who Leave Per Year on Average	20	15	
Above number x 68%	14	10	
Potential Money Saved from Appreciation Events (Above number times Lifetime Value)	**$3500/ Year**	**$24,000/ Year**	

By the way, this is only *one* way of making money from an event, and it takes time and can seem theoretical or intangible. There are actually four ways to make money from an event, which I will cover in the next tip, and my favorite one is *instant, tangible, and very profitable.*

Tip #2: 4 Ways to Make Money From an Event

Would you believe me if I told you that you could put together a lavish event – complete with food, beverages, and fantastic entertainment – all in a sophisticated venue for 100-200 of your best customers (the more, the better), completely FREE without stealing money or charging your customers an admission fee?

If your answer was a big "NO," I wouldn't blame you. It seems hard to believe that you could accomplish putting together a no-corners-cut event for your customers without spending hundreds or even thousands of dollars.

But I've found a way. In fact, I've found four, and there are advantages to each.

4 Ways to Plan an Event for Free:

1. Charge a Ticket Price: For some events, this is a totally viable method of funding an event. But because this is a book about customer appreciation events, I don't recommend it at all. Again, you're trying to show them how much you care, not make them spend more money than necessary in the process.

2. Increased Customer Retention: We talked about this in Tip #1 – know the lifetime value of your average customer. If you compare your annual customer churn (the amount of customers who stop doing business with you) from before you hosted your event to the year after your event and you see a decrease, you just made money. Frankly, there's no clear-cut way of being certain that this decreased churn rate is due solely to your event, but it probably didn't hurt it (remember: 68% of customers leave because they don't feel appreciated enough). If our florist Tracy from before saves just four of the fourteen customers who typically leave her business each year, she saves $1000. Does that pay for her event? It just might! See tip #24 for more ways of measuring these things.

3. Offers at the Event: This needs to be done with a bit of finesse. You don't want to give your customers the impression that you invited them to a sales pitch. This may simply be something you add into the gift-bags your customers get at the end (more on this in Tip #22). The key to making an offer to your customers at your event is to position it as an exclusive opportunity you're extending to them alone to reward them for attending. You could even do a "Groupon" type offer where you give them your regular service at a lowered fee, but they must pay for the voucher in advance. If you can get 50 customers to take a $100 deal, you have $5000 you didn't have before. Or you can make it easier and get 10 customers to take a $500 deal. Up to you!

Another type of "offer" is to ask all of the attendees for a referral to someone like them that you can follow up with as a prospect. If Tracy converts 4 people referred to her at her event, she makes $1000 over the lifetime of those customers.

4. Sponsorships:

I'm sure you have been to charity events where the whole thing is funded by people who pay or donate their services in order to be on a banner or have their information included in the programs. You can do the **same thing** as a for-profit organization!

The short answer on how to find sponsors is to find potential joint venture partners — people who have the same customers as you — and write a sales sequence to ask them to become sponsors at your event, with a focus on the marketing benefits for them.

The more customers you invite, the more you will be able to make in sponsorships. Businesses want to get in front of as many potential customers as possible, so the more people who attend, the more money a sponsor will be willing to spend.

By using a combination of the above strategies (minus #1), you can fully fund your event, and in many cases even turn a profit. If your event costs you $2500 and you make $5000 between sponsorships, people taking offers, referrals, and your increased retention, you've already paid for next year's event! Now you can let that snowball and outdo yourself year after year!

> Sponsorships are a lengthy topic that I can't possibly cover in the full detail I'd like to in this book. If you want to know more about sponsorships, how to structure them, and how to find sponsors, see the offer on page 46.

Tip #3: Design the Event for Sponsors...

Let's talk briefly about sponsors, because this is something a lot of business owners feel nervous about including in their event.

There's no logical reason to pay for your whole

event yourself. You have a list of targeted customers who also use the services of other non-competing businesses. You might even have existing relationships with these businesses, which makes asking them to sponsor that much easier.

For example, if you're a realtor, your customer-base is full of home-owners. **You know who else works with homeowners?** *Landscapers, electricians, plumbers, carpet cleaners, and so much more.*

Do you think that those businesses would love to get in front of your customers? Heck yes! So charge them to do it.

(Important side note about sponsors: You need to screen and vet your potential sponsors. They're paying you to endorse them to your customers. That means that everything those sponsors do with your customers reflects on you. If a customer gets burned by a company they met at your event, they're going to link that to your business.)

If you're going to include sponsors in your event, and I definitely recommend that you do, then it needs to not be an after-thought. The sponsors should be at the forefront of your mind the entire time you're planning, just as important as your customers.

Every step of the way while planning your event, you need to ask yourself the question: "How can I tweak this to deliver more value to my sponsors?"

I'll give you an example. Every year, I host what I call my "VIP Event" for the most important people in my business: clients, partners, vendors, friends, etc.

The theme of my event was a Family Feud game-show night, and as I planned my event, I made sure to think about my sponsors every step of the way.

The result? Three sponsorship levels. The lowest level (which I called the Howie Mandel level, no offense to Howie), included a business card in every gift bag. The middle level (Regis Philbin) included a business card as well as a half-page ad.

The top level (Johnny Carson, appropriately at 6x the price of the lowest level) included the following: A business card and full page ad in the gift bags, an inclusion in the invitations and all event-related emails, their logo on an exclusive vinyl event banner, their logo on all of the nametags and a VIP nametag for themselves, a 3 minute speaking opportunity, inclusion in the thank-you-note to attendees, a Facebook plug, and they were even included as one of the two "families" when we played Family Feud.

Look closely...I included that top sponsor in *every aspect* of the event, and it was easy.

What I did was choreograph the entire event in my mind and put it step-by-step on paper, from the first contact to my customers to the last point of contact related to the event. Then for each of these steps I listed a way that the sponsors could be included.

Contact started with the invitations, so I included the sponsors on those (see page 17)

The next thing my customers would experience were follow-up emails getting them to RSVP and reminding them about the event. So I put the top sponsors in the sidebar with links to their websites.

At the event, the first thing they would get was a nametag, and they'd be looking at those all night, so I threw the sponsors on there.

I think you get the idea. It's not rocket-science. Deliver maximum value to your sponsors at every turn, and they'll come back year after year.

And guess what? Because of the way I designed

the Family Feud game, I could only have two top-level sponsorships (exclusivity is a good thing), and both slots were taken within 2 minutes of the email being sent. I *think* those sponsors saw the value in what I was offering.

Tip #4:...But be Sneaky About It

Like I mentioned earlier, you don't want your valued customers to feel like they've been invited to a sales pitch, so you need to be sneaky about how you include sponsors.

One thing I did with my event to avoid giving

COLLIN STOVER
MAGIC & MENTALISM
VIP 2015

"Come on down!" to the second annual Collin Stover: Magic & Mentalism VIP NIGHT!

Join me in celebrating YOU and all that you have done over the past two years to help me in my business!

With great people like you around me, it's like I've hit the Jackpot! Come on down on April 6th for light appetizers, cash bar, and a hilariously fun game of Family Feud!

Please visit tiny.cc/vip15 to let me know if you are coming or not, either way.

Hosted by Top Hat IMC and Dionne Malush, Realtor
tophat-imc.com   dionnemalush.com

Details:
Date: Monday, April 6th, 2015
Time: 6:00-9:00
Location: Willow
634 Camp Horne Rd,
Pittsburgh, PA 15237
Dress: Business Casual

Here's What You Need To Do:
STEP 1: Visit www.tiny.cc/vip15 to let me know if you are coming or not.

STEP 2: Reserve up to two free tickets for you and one guest.

STEP 3: Meet us at 6:00 at Willow for the **Red Carpet** opening along with exclusive on-time door prizes (Family Feud starts at 7:00)

Include sponsors in as many aspects of your event as possible

17

people a bad taste in their mouths was remove all instances of the word "sponsor" and replace it with "host". As you can see, on the invitations, I said "hosted by _____". The beautiful thing is that this isn't a lie: Because the two Family Feud family names are named after those sponsors, it's like they're hosting the game. In fact, when I had them do their 3 minute speaking slot, it was within the context of "getting to know the families." It was somewhat tongue in cheek, but people enjoyed it a lot more than "here's a word from our sponsors." They paid attention more, too, which made the sponsors happy. It also forced the sponsors to get creative with their speech instead of just delivering a sales pitch.

There's an art to creating marketing opportunities for your sponsors without making your customers feel sold to, but it only takes a little bit of creativity and ingenuity.

Tip #5: Theme It

So far I've told you about my 2015 VIP event, where the theme was a game show night. The year before I did a spy-themed event. Cocktail attire, a candy-cigarette girl, and all in a venue that looked like it came out of a Bond film.

Your customers go to so many boring events and meetings, especially if you're in business to business. People like themes.

You might be saying to yourself, "my customers are too sophisticated for themes," or, "I'm trying to run a serious business!" That's nonsense. Your customers want to have fun. To put it bluntly, they want to forget about their everyday lives. The office, the kids, etc. Themes are a great distraction, and they're more fun to plan.

Let me ask you this: Aside from a cigarette girl, was there much difference between my spy-themed event and a normal event? Not really. In fact, I went to an event about a year previously at the same venue, and it was about the same. I just added an extra element that I think made it more fun (and my guests agree).

More importantly, the spy theme drew people in to attend more than if I wouldn't have themed it. Themes rarely hurt attendance, and they don't typically cost anything extra to implement if you can get creative.

> **DIY:**
> If you're creative, you can do-it-yourself a lot of the things on your list. For example, the cigarette girl was composed of two parts: the cigarette box with the candy cigarettes, and the girl herself. The box we made ourselves using scrap wood and lining it with felt, and the cigarette girl was a friend of mine that I just paid $20 and gave free food. Extremely cost-effective.

Tip #6: Invest in an Event Planner

I can't emphasize enough how great it is to put someone who is an expert in event planning in charge of your event. I've done it on several occasions, but abandoned it because I wanted to develop the event planning skills myself.

There are two ways you can utilize an event planner at your event: (A) a full Event Planner or (B) a Day of Coordinator.

If you invest in someone to plan your whole event, they'll meet with you to discuss your event, what you want to accomplish, and will work with you to create an event that is in line with your goals. They'll take as much of the planning off of your hands as you want – from budgeting, to finding and securing vendors, and running the event. With all of this coordination, however, comes a price. It could be well worth it, though, because this is all time that you aren't spending on planning the event yourself (which gives you time to work on making money in your business), and you aren't taking someone in your company away from their daily tasks.

A Day of Coordinator is a little different – they don't work with you in the planning stages of your event, but as their name suggests, they will be there on the day of the event to make sure everything runs smoothly. This allows you to focus on your guests and facilitating the networking experience, which is really what you should be doing. There are a lot of business owners out there who spend all of the time at their event worrying about if things are running smoothly – so much so that their guests never even get to see them. That makes me ask...what was the point of having the event?

Tip #7: The First Step is Visualization

The first step in planning your event is to sit down in a quiet room with no distractions, silence your phone, lock the door, and grab a pen and a piece of paper (technology disconnects our thoughts).

Next, I want you to close your eyes, breathe deeply for 30 seconds, and then think about what you want your event to be. What do you want your guests to experience? What result do you want to achieve? What thoughts, feelings, or ideas do you want your guests to have while they're there? What about after the event is over? How do you want the event to be themed?

Write down your answers to all of these questions, and **do not censor yourself**. This is the most important thing. Keep writing. Keep the pen moving. Don't stop to think. As soon as you say "no, that's stupid, I'm not going to write that down," your brain says "Okay, filter out ideas," and you draw a blank.

Tackle each of these questions, writing down as many possible solutions as you can. Once you run out of steam, only then should you look at what you wrote and begin making connections and choosing which ideas you'll scrap and what you might want to explore further.

Once you've done this first exercise, you should then close your eyes and "teleport" yourself to your event. Imagine what it will be like to walk in. What do you see? What do you smell? What do you hear? Create the event from start to finish in your mind. Then write it all down.

This exercise in total takes 30-45 minutes, but it's so vital to the success of your event. This initial visualization creates a "blueprint" for your event that you can use while moving forward to create a formal agenda. Knowing what you want your event to look like also assists you in finding a venue, entertainment, and other vendors, because you'll know from your visualization if someone fits in with the types of feelings and experiences you want your guests to have.

Tip #8: Leave Nothing to Chance (but be Flexible)

Now that you have a plan, you can create your formal agenda.

I could write a whole other book on how to create an agenda and plan the logistics of your event, but instead of doing that, I've created a whole program dedicated to it. If you're interested in learning more about that program, see the offer on page 64.

The most important thing to remember is that all parts of your event should be scheduled down to the last minute. Even "down time" where your guests are just networking with each other (which is very important to include) needs to be scheduled and facilitated so that the guests don't feel like it was unplanned filler.

All of this being said, you also need to be flexible. Your event is never going to run *perfectly*. I'll use my 2014 event as an example – the spy-themed cocktail party. It was originally supposed to be a casino night with a spy theme. We checked with the venue several times to make sure it would be okay, and they gave verbal statements that they thought the casino night sounded really cool and they couldn't wait to have us.

When we got there and started setting up, a new manager we hadn't spoken to yet approached us and told us that we couldn't play casino games because they had a bar, and the law in Pennsylvania says that without a special license, you can't gamble in a bar (even though we weren't playing for money).

Extremely disappointed at first, we had just 10 minutes before people started showing up to come up with a new way to entertain them. Luckily, I'm pretty quick on my feet, so we came up with a fun networking game to play which connected everybody in the room and got everyone acquainted and talking to each other.

It wasn't a casino night, but the backup plan worked.

I'm a big listener of National Public Radio, and it's usually what's playing when I'm in the car. Just yesterday as I was listening, on two separate occasions, there was some kind of technical mistake. The first time, they played the wrong soundbyte, and I assume they couldn't locate the right one. Amazingly, the host simply said "That wasn't _____," and went right onto the next thing without a beat. It doesn't get much more scheduled than syndicated radio, but she was flexible enough to implement that back-up plan (which I'm sure she had sitting by for in-case-of-emergency situations).

Being flexible and having a backup plan for when the inevitable happens can be the difference between coming off to your guests as prepared and professional, or unprepared and inept.

Tip #9: Book the Venue First (Then Entertainment)

Once you have a theme and an agenda, it's time to find a venue. The reason you book the venue first is threefold:

(A) The venue is going to be the thing that is booked up the farthest in advance.

(B) The venue is such an integral part to accommodating your theme, that once you find the "perfect" one, you're going to want to secure it before someone else sweeps in and takes your date.

(C) You can't book much else if you don't have a venue to tell them.

There are various ways to go about finding a venue. At this point you should have an idea of how many people you are inviting and how many you expect will show up. Can you have your party in the back room of a restaurant? Do you need to move up to a banquet hall?

Restaurants tend to be cheaper, because they usually don't charge to rent the room, they just have a minimum order. Banquet halls usually charge for the room *and* if you have them cater the event.

As an entertainer, I've been to all kinds of venues for all kinds of celebrations. What I can tell you is that the events that felt more lively were ones where the room was *slightly* too small to accommodate every person who attended. In a sit-down dinner situation, you obviously need seating for everyone. But if you're just doing a cocktail party, not everyone needs a seat at all times.

On the contrary, when I've been to events where the room was too *big*, it spread people out and no one talked to each other. It also seemed like there were less people there than if you would have crammed everybody into a smaller room. Big rooms force people into their own safe corners of the world. Small rooms force people to bump into each other and network.

When choosing the perfect venue, keep in mind where your customers live, how they will park, where they'll be coming from, etc.

After the venue, you should secure your entertainment. I know that sounds self-serving, but it's for a reason. The entertainment is going to be what people remember most about your event. Plain and simple. There was a study done (which, admittedly, was for weddings, but applies here as well) that said that 80% of guests remember the entertainment most (*St. Louis Bride and Groom Magazine*, 2003). With this much riding on the entertainment, you don't want to wait too long and get who's *left*, you want the *best* person for your event.

How soon should you book entertainment? It depends on the time of year, but I'd say as soon as you know the venue. In December and January, I'm many times booked a year in advance for prime dates. August? It might just be a few months in advance.

> **This *is* self-serving:** I'm not the best fit for every event, however I *have* performed for thousands of happy adults at events ranging from Pittsburgh Steeler fundraiser galas, NHL weddings, and fortune 500 company events. If you're interested in featuring a sophisticated magic and mentalism experience (either walking around in the crowd or up in stage in front of everyone at once) at your event, like these folks were, please visit collinstover. com/QuickTipsMagic

Tip #10: How to Avoid Being ROBBED By Vendors

Imagine the perfect event: full attendance, happy guests, great food and drinks. People approach you left and right to tell you how appreciative they are and how they're going to be customers for LIFE!

The day suddenly takes a turn for the worst, as men in masks crash through the windows and doors and demand all of the money in the room. *You're being robbed at your own event.*

Okay, so it doesn't usually happen like that, unless we're in a *Quentin Tarantino* flick, but there's a different kind of robbery that you have to look out for when it comes to your event – and it happens all the time.

Unreliable, Unscrupulous, Untrustworthy Vendors.

It's likely you don't have too much experience working with event vendors – after all, we only hold these events once a year at most. There are some people who take advantage of this fact, and prey upon business owners, taking down-payments and never showing up, not delivering what was promised, or worse.

Perhaps the worst part isn't that a vendor took your money and ran — it's that now there's a piece missing from your event that your guests won't get to experience. Just imagine if your DJ decided to hit the road before your event, which was supposed to be full of dancing!

There are 6 ways to avoid dealing with untrustworthy vendors, and ultimately avoid being robbed on the day of your event:

1. Get an Event Planner: This is the easiest way to avoid being "had" by your vendors. A planner has worked with the best in your city, and her neck is on the line if you get ripped off. Of course, you need to follow the rest of these tips to find a trustworthy planner, because even that business has hacks and rip-offs.

2. Read Online Reviews Carefully: The nature of the Internet is that anyone can write anything as anyone. I'd recommend that if you aren't sure, ask for references and/or ask to speak to their last 3 clients on the phone. If they don't want you to do that, you should hear alarm bells.

3. Opt for the In-Person Meeting: I know, we're all busy, but meeting a vendor in person before signing anything is a great idea for a few reasons. (A) you'll be able to see if your personalities mesh well, (B) you'll be able to tell a lot easier if they're faking it (although some people are remarkably good fakers), and (C) you can get a demonstration of what they have to offer at your event. If a vendor won't meet with you in person, move on to the next person on your list. They aren't going to be worth the trouble.

4. ALWAYS Get a Contract: If a vendor is working without the use of contracts, run the other direction as fast as you can. Without a written agreement, it's much more difficult to prove any kind of transaction took place. A contract, at the very least, serves as a blueprint that you can refer to when things aren't being delivered as promised.

5. The Best Source of Vendors: Referrals: I still maintain that the best way to find vendors for your event is through a referral from someone you know, like, and trust.

That means friends, family, business partners, other vendors you've worked with successfully, etc. They're putting their neck out there when they refer someone, so they aren't going to refer you to someone who is going to do a poor job.

6. Trust Your Gut: Always trust your gut reactions to vendors. If you get a "bad feeling" after talking to someone, it's probably for a reason. **Don't ignore it!**

In the Internet age, you would think finding people to host, cater, photograph, and entertain your event would be easy. Quite the contrary: the sheer amount of choices out there makes choosing "the right one" paralyzing. Anyone with an Internet connection and $7 a month can set up a site and essentially own their own business.

I can't say that I recommend simply Googling someone or looking them up in the Yellow Pages. If you do go this route, be sure to follow all of the above rules to avoid being burned.

Tip #11: The Pros and Cons of Working With Talent Agencies

Essentially a one-stop-shop for all things party and entertainment, talent agencies are like the retailers of the entertainment industry. They carry a "stock" of entertainers and vendors (magicians, DJs, photographers, videographers, etc.) for whom they pay wholesale for, so that their customers can have the convenience of finding everything in one place instead of shopping around. Talent agencies can be found in every major city, and there are certainly benefits as well as drawbacks to working with them.

The first, and most obvious benefit to working with a talent agency is the fact that they do all of the work for you. You simply call them up, tell them what you want, what your budget is, and they'll find a match. You could call and say, "I have $2000, I need a magician, a DJ, and a balloon artist," and they'll call their contacts to find people willing to do it for a total of $2000.

Secondly, there's less back-end work involved, as you'll typically sign one agreement with the talent agency, give them one check, and they'll settle up with the vendors. This can create less stress on the day of your event, because you don't have to worry about who needs paid and when.

Unfortunately there are some major drawbacks to working with talent agencies, which you may or may not mind depending on your priorities for your event.

In order to explain the drawbacks, I need to explain how talent agencies work. A client calls an agency with a need and a budget. The agency then calls several entertainers and asks if they have the date open. If they do have the date open, the talent agency quotes a price lower than your budget, because that's how they make their money. In many cases a talent agency will add 25-50% on top of what they're actually paying the entertainer. You're paying the same price you probably would otherwise, but the entertainer isn't getting their full fee.

Why is this a problem for you if you're still paying the same fee? It comes down to quality. Let's say, for example, your budget is $1200 for a DJ (a made-up number). If you go straight to a DJ, minus the entertainment agency, you might find a great, quality DJ for that amount. **When you go to an agency, however, you're getting a DJ who's willing to do it for $600 instead of $1200, but you're still paying the $1200 price tag** for the convenience of not doing the research yourself. A good DJ is going to charge what they're worth. Unfortunately the people who do a lot of work for talent agencies are simply "weekend warriors" who have a day job and just do this for some extra cash on the weekends. That might be great for your event, but you're paying the price tag for a full-time DJ with lots of experience, and you're getting someone who values their time much less than that. That could, but doesn't always mean that they will be of lesser quality. That's the risk you're taking.

Another drawback is the fact that many agencies don't really care who is the best fit for your event. They hear "$1200" and "DJ" and they hook you up with someone who can accommodate. In my experience, many agencies don't even know a lot about the vendors they work with. They just care about the price they can get them down to. This isn't all agencies – there are certainly reasonable and helpful agencies out there. However I've found that in my experience these types are the minority.

Finally, you can't build a relationship with the professionals you invest in through the agency. This may not be important to you, but it can be nice sometimes to develop a relationship with an entertainer with whom you can work with again and again, refer to your friends, etc. With an agency, you usually don't even get the entertainer's last name, and each time you want to work with that person, you have to do so through the agency.

So, the question is, should you use a talent agency? I give a similar answer for many questions: <u>do what is best for you and your event.</u>

If convenience is your primary concern, then perhaps you should go to an agency (although personally, I think it would be more worth it to invest in an event planner, who will do a better job researching the entertainment while staying within your budget – See Tip #6). If quality and value for your money is a priority, then you should either invest in an event planner, do the research yourself, or ask someone you trust for a referral. I connect many of my clients with other event professionals that I have worked with in the past who I know will do a great job, and I don't charge a fee to do so.

Tip #12: The Best Times to Have an Event

When I say the best "times" to have an event, I'm referring to three things: the time of year, the time of week, and the time of day.

Depending on what time of year you have your event, it's going to dictate when you send out invitations. For example, December is extremely busy for people. They have family functions to go to, shopping to do, their own company holiday parties, and holiday parties they get invited to by people like you. Because of this, you need to try to get on their schedule with ample time to spare if you want them to attend.

I'm a fan of January holiday parties, and they're very well attended, because most of the holiday rush has ended.

On the flip side, in June and July, you have a lot of people on vacation. Just keep these things in mind when planning your event.

There are also advantages and disadvantages to certain days of the week. Weekends are popular for events, but the problem is that venues charge more for these prime spots. Weeknights are great because the venue charges less, and people can many times come straight from work to your event, which is convenient for your guests.

I've been to events on weekends and weeknights, and I can't tell if either one is more attended than another.

For time of day, it depends if you're serving dinner

or not, and if it's on a weekend or not. A weekday at 4:00 isn't going to work, because people are still at work. Similarly, you can't keep everyone there until 12:00 AM on a weekday when people have to get up early in the morning.

On weekends you have a little more flexibility. If you're serving dinner, you could start the event at 4:30 or 5:00. If you expect people to already have eaten dinner, I'd recommend starting it no earlier than 6:00.

The time to have your event also depends on who your guests are. Do they have kids who have after-school activities or that they need to find babysitters for? Do they mostly work from home on a flexible schedule, or do they work in an office from 9-5?

By the way, there's a fine line between inviting people early enough, and inviting people too early that they forget about the event. Find that balance. In most cases, I recommend at least a month before the event date. For holiday parties, you might want to bump that up to September or October, depending on who your guests are.

Save the Date:

One way to avoid sending invitations too early or too late is to send a "Save the Date" email to let them know that you intend to invite them to an event on your date. That way you allow people to put it in their calendar before you actually send the formal invitations.

Tip #13: Who to Invite

There's a simple answer to the question, "Who should I invite?": as many as you can afford. These events work because lots of people are getting together to celebrate and talk about your business. Sponsorships work because businesses want to get in front of as many targeted people as possible. Therefore, the more the merrier.

You can also choose whether or not to allow people to bring a guest. At my events, about 90% of people elected to bring their significant other or a friend, so factor that into your attendance when choosing food and venue.

It' really up to you who you invite. Just keep in

mind that the more people you invite, the higher the investment is going to be initially, but you'll also have a higher return-on-investment.

Tip #14: Paper Invitations vs. E-Vites

Invitations have changed *a lot* in the past 10 years or so. With sites like Eventbrite, Evite, and even Facebook, there's a booming trend in E-vites as opposed to sending a hard copy invitation. More and more, businesses are turning to the Internet as a means of saving some cash on the printing and posting of physical invitations.

While there are no official studies done on the effectiveness of one type vs. the other, surveying event planners has revealed to me that there really is no advantage or disadvantage as far as RSVP rate goes. Consumer surveys also show that the two forms are head to head for number of people using each type of invitation. So why use one over the other?

There's nothing inherently *wrong* with E-vites, and for some events they are perfectly acceptable. What I will ask you to think about, though, is which is more memorable?

I can tell you that personally, I can remember just about every business event I've ever gotten a physical invitation to. They make me feel important and appreciated when I see that stamp in the corner. Someone *paid* to invite me to something (which shouldn't be that special for me, since I get paid to attend events as the entertainment for my living). There's no doubt that there's a feeling of excitement when you open up that envelope. It's like a little gift amongst all of the bills and junk mail.

E-vites simply don't give me that same feeling, and I suspect that you and your customers feel the same way. So the bottom line is that while your response rate probably won't suffer if you send out an E-vite, your customers will certain feel more appreciated if you opt for the physical mail at an additional cost.

Tip #15: What to Include on Invitations

There's some important information that should be included in any business event invitation. **Make sure your invitations cover all of these bases:**

1. Date and time

2. Location and directions

3. Suggested attire

4. What will be served (Dinner? Light appetizers? Cash bar or comped? Etc.)

5. A brief description of what to expect at the event (why do they want to come?)

6. How to RSVP

7. **BONUS:** Not necessary, but I like to include very specific, step-by-step instructions as to what I want them to do. See the image example from my 2014 event below as an example.

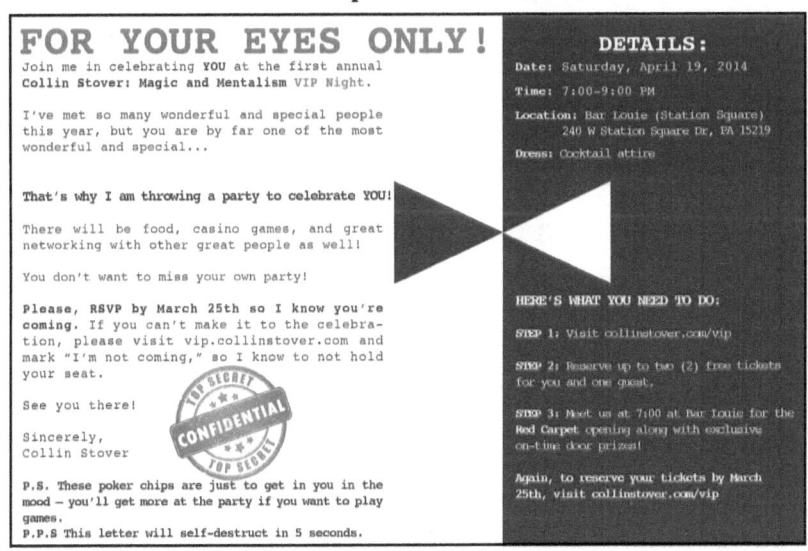

FOR YOUR EYES ONLY!

Join me in celebrating YOU at the first annual
Collin Stover: Magic and Mentalism VIP Night.

I've met so many wonderful and special people
this year, but you are by far one of the most
wonderful and special...

That's why I am throwing a party to celebrate YOU!

There will be food, casino games, and great
networking with other great people as well!

You don't want to miss your own party!

**Please, RSVP by March 25th so I know you're
coming.** If you can't make it to the celebra-
tion, please visit vip.collinstover.com and
mark "I'm not coming," so I know to not hold
your seat.

See you there!

Sincerely,
Collin Stover

P.S. These poker chips are just to get in you in the
mood — you'll get more at the party if you want to play
games.
P.P.S This letter will self-destruct in 5 seconds.

DETAILS:

Date: Saturday, April 19, 2014

Time: 7:00-9:00 PM

Location: Bar Louie (Station Square)
240 W Station Square Dr, PA 15219

Dress: Cocktail attire

HERE'S WHAT YOU NEED TO DO:

STEP 1: Visit collinstover.com/vip

STEP 2: Reserve up to two (2) free tickets
for you and one guest.

STEP 3: Meet us at 7:00 at Bar Louie for the
Red Carpet opening along with exclusive
on-time door prizes!

Again, to reserve your tickets by March
25th, visit collinstover.com/vip

8 Tips for Making your Invitation Stick Out, Get Opened, and Get Remembered by Your Customers

1. A Colored Envelope: Don't be boring! A nice bright color that fits in with the theme of your event will do wonderfully. People *welcome* these kinds of envelopes into their mailbox because they know it's not a bill.

True story: I send a printed newsletter out every month to my very best clients. One of my clients explained to me that every month, her husband hand-delivers her my newsletter because it's in a bright red envelope, and he says, "it must be important". I would assume that he's not the only one who thinks that.

2. Hand-Written (or fake hand-written) address information: Not only are these opened more often, they're actually *delivered* more often. An exposé into the postal industry revealed that mass-mailings that appeared as if they wouldn't be missed (i.e. tons of mailings from the same address with printed addresses) had a tendency to "fall of the truck" more often than mailings with hand-written information. You can always pay some kids $10/hour to write these. If you can't find a kid and you don't feel like writing them yourself, you can always use a *nice* and *realistic* (read: *not* Comic Sans) handwriting font, but that's not ideal. Real hand-written envelopes make your customers feel important.

3. Lumpy Mail: Lumpy mail, or 3D mail as it is sometimes called, is mail that has something in it. These *always* get delivered and *always* get opened because people are dying to know what is inside. For my 2014 appreciation event (casino night), I sent a poker chip. It just gave it a bit more weight and girth that made sure *everyone* opened it. **WARNING:** Because lumpy mail cannot be put through the machines that the post office uses for standard flat mail, you will be required to place extra postage on it. Most light packages will be upgraded to $.70, but make sure you get it checked out by the post office. I made this mistake once early on, and some of my customers were billed for the difference when their mail person arrived! How embarrassing for me!

4. Real Stamps: Real stamps outperform inked stamps every time in A/B split tests. And *multiple* stamps outperform single stamps. If your postage is going to be $.70, perhaps you should place a $.49 and a $.21 stamp on each instead of a single $.70 stamp. Mail with multiple stamps has a higher perceived value.

5. Creative Copy: Don't be boring with what you write on the inside. Make your customers *want* to RSVP! Give them a taste of what they'll experience, and leave a little mystery as well (see the image on page 42)

6. Step-by-Step Instructions: Tell your customers *exactly* what you want them to do. In your invitation, they should know what to wear, where to park, how to get there, how to RSVP, etc.

7. Easy RSVPs: Make RSVPing for your event easy. People are busy. If they perceive that this is going to be a difficult or time-consuming process, they won't bother. I recommend creating an easy URL on your website (for example, yourdomain.com/VIP) and putting a simple form on that page. Set it up so that when they RSVP they're immediately added to an email newsletter list and are emailed with a copy of the details.

You could also give an option to RSVP via phone, however this is best if you have an assistant, so you don't personally have your work interrupted by the influx of phone calls. If you don't have an assistant and would still like to give people the option to RSVP, you could use a tool like MyRSVPLive which will handle all of your RSVPs (and invitations, if you're inclined to go the EVite route) and allow guests to RSVP via phone without you actually answering.

8. Follow-Up: Follow up with your guests as you approach the event with reminders (more in the next chapter).

Tip # 16: Follow Up with Your Invitees

There are two kinds of follow up to your invitations: Follow up to RSVPs, and Follow up to Non-RSVPs.

With the first kind, you're going to send emails on a weekly or biweekly basis to people who RSVPed that they will be there, reminding them about the event and getting them excited about it. This way they won't forget to show up.

For the second group, you're going to send emails on a weekly or biweekly basis to get them to RSVP. Sending emails with subjects like "Will I see you on {Month} {Day}?" are effective. You don't want to bug them, but you want to keep sending emails until they either RSVP or tell you that they can't make it.

For both of these, you can use a free email management program like Mailchimp to segment your guest list into groups (people who RSVPed as attending, people who RSVPed as not attending, and people who haven't RSVPed) to send targeted emails depending on what groups your guests are in.

There's an art to writing these emails and making them entertaining. I'm a fan of telling stories when I write letters to people. The story draws them in, and then I can deliver my message. See the below final email that was sent to people who didn't RSVP for my 2015 VIP event.

Dear {NAME},

Did you know that hummingbirds snore?

I didn't believe it until I got a Facebook "share" from Kaelin last week. It was perhaps the cutest thing ever. Click here to watch that video if you don't believe me.

Neither Kaelin nor I snore on a regular basis, however there was one time I can remember when she was sick and her airways were blocked, and it caused the poor thing to snore awfully.

At the time, I wasn't thinking "you poor thing," or "look at my little hummingbird" – I was thinking, "I want to sleep!"

I'm sure if you have a partner who snores, you know the feeling. It's this feeling like you're angry at them because you want to sleep, but you know it's nothing they're doing on purpose or even conscious

---

of. It's quite a situation.

So I did what came naturally...I nudged her so she'd wake up just enough to stop snoring for a moment. Of course, in a few moments, she'd be back at it and I'd be back at curling a pillow around my head and praying for something to fall through the roof and knock me unconscious so I could get some sleep.

Finally, I decided enough was enough, and went downstairs to sleep on the couch.

Then something amazing happened. She got up on her own, went to the bathroom, blew her nose, took some medicine, and returned to bed. I waited a few minutes...**no more snoring**.

I hurriedly rushed up to bed so I could get to sleep before it would start again, and I finally got the rest I was looking for.

She's my little hummingbird...

Now {NAME}, I've been *nudging* you for the past two weeks to RSVP for my 2015 "VIP Event," where I treat my very best clients, partners, and friends to excellent food and fun in order to show my appreciation for all that they do to help make me successful. (Click here to RSVP)

So far, from what I can tell, I've gotten your attention with my nudges just enough for you stop for a moment, but you still haven't decided to take me up on my invitation.

I'm deciding to do what I did with Kaelin...I'm going to leave you alone.

This will be my final email about RSVPing. I'll leave the ball in your court. It's totally up to you whether you want to come or not.

What I can tell you is that I'm inviting 50 of the people most important to my business, and you're one of those people, so I would love to have you there.

But, alas, I need to give a final number to the venue for how many people I'm expecting. So by 8 AM tomorrow, I have to close the doors on this offer.

Click here to RSVP (or to at least let me know that you can't make it)

I hope to see you there!

Magically Yours,

Collin

Tip #17: Use Ambiance to Create an Unforgettable Sensory Experience

I want you to imagine walking into your grandmother's house as a child. Remember the smells of a fresh baking pie or home-cooked meal. Remember what everything looked like. Remember the sounds — maybe of conversation, maybe of a TV or radio playing. If you're someone who frequently visited grandma's house when you were little, I immediately took you back there, and that evoked a lot of feelings. Feelings of warmth, feelings of nostalgia, and maybe even some bittersweet emotions as well.

This is what our senses do to us, and this is what you want to create for your guests. Use your theme, the venue, and your vision for what you want your guests to feel, to create a sensory *experience*.

Ambiance isn't just decorations. It's the combination of all of our senses firing at once, which stirs up emotions, either good or bad, about what we're experiencing. If your event doesn't have entertainment, if it's in a bland room, if the sounds are of people murmuring to each other instead of having a good time, then it's going to be a bad experience.

If instead, your guests walk into a room full of the sounds of happy, chatty people; the smell of great food being prepared; and the sight of people hugging and shaking hands in a beautifully decorated room; it will be a positive experience.

Tip #18: Keep Education Interesting

For many events, there is an educational portion that can't be avoided. Usually this just means the owner gets up and thanks everybody, maybe talks about some new innovations in his/her business, or reveals plans for the upcoming year. This is all fine and good, and it's somewhat expected by your guests.

But please, for the love of all that is holy, do not wing it. *Prepare* a speech, and deliver it expertly. If you are not a good speaker, keep your comments short and delegate the rest of the speaking to someone who is. If you're going to stand there and say "um" and "uh" and "y'know" then don't even get out of your seat.

I can't tell you how many events I've been to that were going so well until someone got up to speak. Instantly, the credibility of the person who put together the event went down, because it sounded like they didn't know anything about anything.

Keep in mind that an educational portion can interrupt the "flow" of the event. Plan it at a time when people are captive and politely chatting (like right before dinner, for example). Don't interrupt dancing or other activities with your speech, because people might not be able to get back into the groove.

That's about all I have to say about the educational portion: Keep it short, and keep it entertaining. Talk as if you actually *like* your company and are excited about the year ahead. Brainstorm ways you can make it more interesting. One team-appreciation event I was performing at put together a skit for before the short educational portion. It wasn't the best skit, of course, but it was funny, and that was what was important. It got people's attention, got them laughing, and kept them from yawning through the rest of the presentation.

Tip #19: Include Something for Everyone

If you have a diverse range of guests coming, you need to keep in mind that they all have different likes and interests, and that you need to accommodate every one of them. For example, if the primary form of entertainment is dancing to a DJ, what are the non-dancers going to do?

In cases such as these, perhaps you should consider including some kind of interactive entertainment so that they don't feel left out. If you're doing a seating chart, maybe you can put the people who you feel certain will dance at tables together, and people who don't dance at the other tables. That way no one will be left there sitting alone while everyone else dances. Just a thought.

There are lots of ways to entertain non-dancers, including: photobooths, magicians, table games, balloon twisters, psychics/palm readers, jugglers, fire-spitters, belly-dancers, and more.

Tip #20: Craft a Grand Entrance

What your guests experience when they arrive to your event is a most critical part of how they will remember the night.

There are some logistical objectives that need to be met at this part, like registering guests so you know who attended. You also need to consider other things, like:

• If it's winter, what will they do with their coats?

• How do they know what they're supposed to do after they register?

• Are there programs to hand out?

• Will they have name tags? Are they pre-printed, or will they need to be written?

• How will you register people? Paper sheet? Computer? If you're using electronic registration, what will you do if the system fails (like it did for my event planner friend – she had paper backups)

• What do you do if someone brings someone along who was not invited? How will you account for them and follow up with them (maybe you should bring drop-in forms to capture their information)

It's these logistics that make the registration period a mundane part of most business events, and that's a shame, because it's the first thing your guests are going to experience when they arrive.

I don't suggest getting rid of the registration – after all, tracking and measurement is very important in all of this. Instead, I recommend doing it in an interesting way that's different from the way everyone else does it.

Most people experience this when they attend an event: They walk in, someone who doesn't know them greets them at a registration desk and asks them their name, they're signed in, given a name tag or a sticker and a program, and they're on their way in, wandering somewhat aimlessly.

Is there anything interesting, memorable, or comfortable about the above situation? No. It's all uncomfortable, and it's what everyone else is doing.

There are many ways you can make this piece more interesting, and it only takes a bit of creativity.

I'll tell you what I did for my event in 2014: Instead of putting the registration at the forefront of what they experienced, I made it the second step. I went to vistaprint.com and printed out two banners with my logo and the logo I created for my event, and I put them side by side behind a red carpet. The first thing my clients experienced when they walked through the door was a "red carpet treatment."

I greeted them personally by name at the door, shook their hands, and they, their spouse/guest, and I got our pictures taken by a professional photographer on the red carpet. What's even cooler is that at the time of writing this, it's almost a year afterwards and some of these people *still* have these photos set as their Facebook profile pictures. People love any photo of themselves dressed up and without their kids, and I love the free marketing!

After they had their photo taken, I introduced them by name to my "guest coordinator." who signed them in and got them their name tag. The guest coordinator was also scripted to tell them exactly what they should do directly after they were registered, that way they weren't wandering around aimlessly.

Anything you can do to eliminate confusion and/or/make things more interesting, you should do in all areas of your event, but especially in this early stage.

Tip #21: Entertain them While They're There

Here's where the real expert planning takes place. I'm not going to delve into nitty-gritty details here — please refer to my offer on page 64 for more information.

I will give you the golden rule, though, which, if you keep at the forefront of your mind, you'll have an event that your customers will remember and look forward to year after year.

The Golden Rule: Whatever You Do, Break the Ice!

This is the number one thing you need to keep in mind while planning your event. If you make decisions based on this golden rule, you'll be on the right track to planning an unforgettable event.

Let me ask you this: *How many of your guests know each other?*

The likely answer for most industries, is very few.

With that in mind, do you think your guests feel totally comfortable walking into a situation where they don't know anyone, but they have to make friends with the strangers sitting at their table with them?

Unless your customers are all social butterflies (and even then), probably not.

Your #1 job as a party host at this point is to break that ice. Provide them with some activity, form of entertainment, etc. that will allow them to get to know each other in a non-threatening way.

One thing I've seen done at weddings to break the ice amongst families who have never met is they'll include a custom Mad Libs at every table that the guests have to work together to fill in and read. It's entertaining, it's funny, and it gives strangers a jumping off point to start a conversation.

Another way to break the ice is to invest in interactive entertainment. This is what I specialize in at the events I'm paid to perform at.

What I do is walk from table to table and vet groups that I know could use some ice-breaking. Then I perform a 5-10 minute mini-show for them that gets them smiling, laughing, and shouting. By the time I'm finished with them, it's like they're best friends. I love leaving a table who didn't know each other and coming back later in the night to see that they're carrying on as if they had known each other for years.

Here's what one of my clients said in relation to breaking the ice: "I feel my guests will talk about my event for a long time because of the experience they had; I also received the benefit of knowing that my guests enjoyed themselves and got to laugh, be confused, amazed, and meet others they didn't know before the party – because after Collin left their table, they talked to one another about what they just saw."

Tip #22: Say Goodbye (the Right Way)!

If your answer to this question is a swift kick in the rear, don't-let-the-door-hit-you-on-the-way-out, then you've got another thing coming!

Customers are the kings and queens and the judges and the jury in your business, and as such, they should be treated like royalty. That means that at the very least, they should receive a salutations from someone on your staff (preferably you) before they leave.

I would also recommend a gift-bag full of stuff they actually want (not just boring stuff like pens and magnets), because (A) everyone likes gifts and (B) this is where you're going to put some of your sponsor benefits. If it was a bag full of *just* sponsor info, no one would want the bags. If instead it was stuff they could actually use, *plus* sponsor info, they're going to be more likely to look into it and read your sponsors' info.

Tip #23: Say Thank You

How you follow up with the customers who attended your event afterwards says a lot about your business in their minds. If there's *no* follow-up, they probably won't notice (but no one has ever bought from a company they didn't notice).

I would recommend following up in some way, whether it's a card mailed to their house (an email is the bare-minimum version of this, but it doesn't amount to much in the minds of your customers), or a phone call thanking them and asking what they thought.

It's important to figure out what your customers enjoyed most about the event and what they would like to see changed for next year. No event is perfect, and there are always ways of making it better. Asking for honest, uncensored feedback (and rewarding those who give it in some way) is a great way to improve your event year after year. Plus, people are more likely to come to an event if they feel they helped shape it in some way.

I offer a service to my VIP level clients where I'll actually hand-write and address a thank-you card to their specifications to every person on their guest list who attended. That way, the daunting task of thanking everyone is as simple as sending me a list and what they want the cards to say.

Tip #24: Measure the Success of Your Event

As I said in my opening, the measurement marketing efforts is of the utmost importance for all businesses. This extends to your events as well, and there's a formulaic way to measure the success of your event, just as you would measure conversions on a website or calls from a newspaper ad.

Use the table on page 62 (along with the Tracy's Floral example) to calculate the value of your own event. This will give you some helpful metrics for next year, and hopefully will encourage you to continue hosting events on an annual basis.

If you find that you are "in the red" in line N, you should look to increase profits in rows G, J, I, or K for next year. For example, if your number in row J isn't very high, you need to make a better effort next year to secure quality sponsors. If getting sponsors is something you're having a difficult time with, you may want to take a look at my A–Z appreciation event planning program, which I offer to you on page 64.

	Why this is Important	Tracy's Floral	Your Event
A. Number of Invitations Sent	Use these numbers to calculate the following values for future use: Percentage of guests who RSVPed (A ÷ B), Percentage of RSVPs who showed up (B ÷ C) and Percentage of guests who brought a +1 (C ÷ D). You can also use letters A and E to get an idea of how many guests will show up depending on number of invitations sent.	200	
B. Number of RSVPs (Count 1 per household – do not include +1s)		125	
C. Number of invited guests who showed up (not including +1s)		100	
D. Number of +1s who showed up.		50	
E. Total number of guests in attendance (C + D)		150	
F. If you had an offer at the event, how many people took you up on it?	Use E ÷ F to see what percentage of people took you up on your offer. This can help you plan for next year's event.	10 people took Tracy up on her $50 offer.	
G. How much, in total, did you make from your offer?		$500	
H. How many referrals did you receive at the event?	Again, E ÷ H will give you the percentage of guests who gave you referrals.	12 referrals	
I. How many of those referrals did you convert to paying customers? Multiply this number by the lifetime value of a customer (page 4)	After some time has passed, take a tally of how many of those referrals you successfully "converted" into paying customers and multiply it by the lifetime value of your average customer.	6 referrals converted. Lifetime value of one of Tracy's customers is $250. 6 x $250 = $1,500 in referral value.	

	Why this is Important	Tracy's Floral	Your Event
J. How much did you make in sponsorship money?	Money *before* the event!	$550	
K. Next Year: Compare the number of customers who have left your business in previous years to the number of customers who left in the year since hosting your event. Multiply this by the lifetime value of your customer (Page 4)	This metric won't be valid for at least 12 months after your event, so you can leave it out of your total for now. Theoretically (according to Tip #1), the number of customers who leave should decrease by 68%.	Used to lose an average of 20 customers per year. In the year since her event, Tracy only lost 12. 8 (# of customers "saved" by the event) x $250 (lifetime value of her average customer) = $2,000	
L. Add G + I + J + K to arrive at the total gross value of your event		$500 + $1,500 + $550 + $2,000= $4,550	
M. Total event cost:		$3,125	
N. Net Profit from Event (L-M)		**$4,550 – $3,125 = $1425 profit**	

Tip #25: Claim The Most Amazing Free Gift Ever!

I hope this book gave you at least a basic understanding of what goes into planning and executing an appreciation event for your customers that maximizes memorability and return-on-investment.

That being said, I've only just scratched the surface with these basic tips. Instead of going into too much gory detail in this book, I've put together an online program that walks you through planning your own event, step-by-step, from A-Z so that you can maximize your profits without wasting your time learning what the experts already know.

In this online course, I've assembled video, audio, and PDF content full of interviews with event experts, and actionable steps that you can take so that you can start seeing more success in your event planning.

If you wish to plan a successful and profit-producing event for your customers without hiring an event planner, this course is perfect for you. And because you obtained this book, I'm going to give you a very special offer, that you can only claim using the serial code below.

Please visit collinstover.com/QuickTipsProgram and input the serial code below to get the program at a special book-owners value today!

Serial Code: TIAFSCTIEB0915

Entertainment for Your Event

My full-time business is in delivering a sophisticated magic & mentalism experience at events where the primary audience is adults – risk free with complimentary Reactions Photography© included so that you don't have to miss a single priceless reaction from your guests.

If this is something you think you'd be interested in featuring for your guests, please visit:

www.collinstover.com/QuickTipsMagic

About the Author: Collin Stover

Collin Stover is a professional magician and mentalist in Pittsburgh, Pennsylvania, who has performed over the past ten years for thousands of individuals, ranging from Pittsburgh Steelers and Penguins, to Fortune 500 Executives. Collin has been featured on the cover of the Pittsburgh City Paper, KDKA/CBS Pittsburgh, Pittsburgh Today Live, as well as numerous online publications. When he is not amazing guests with his sophisticated magic and mentalism skills or helping his clients maximize the success of their events, he is with the love of his life, Kaelin.

www.ingramcontent.com/pod-product-compliance
Lightning Source LLC
Chambersburg PA
CBHW021906170526
45157CB00005B/1984